ALL VOWELS MATTER

Written by
Sreekanth Kumar
Chakra Sreekanth

Edited by
Sashi Sreekanth

Illustrated by
Emily Zieroth

Copyright © 2019 Sreekanth Kumar

All rights reserved. No part of this book may be reproduced in any form or by any electronic or mechanical means, including information storage and retrieval systems, without permission in writing from the publisher, except by reviewers, who may quote brief passages in a review.

All Vowels Matter
Written by Sreekanth Kumar and Chakra Sreekanth
Edited by Sashi Sreekanth and Tamara Rittershaus
Illustrations by Emily Zieroth

Summary
All Vowels Matter is a story about five vowels – A, E, I, O and U. When shunned by the other vowels, O makes a wish that A, E, I, and U wouldn't be able to use O for a day. The wish comes true, and the inability to use O puts A, E, I and U in awkward situations. They say things that no one understands, baffling themselves, their parents and their teachers. The vowels learn a valuable lesson that a lack of inclusion and acceptance can have an adverse impact on learning. They learn to celebrate diversity because "All Vowels Matter" — no matter how different they are.

All Vowels Matter stays true to the spirit of making learning fun by teaching the parts of speech with a sense of humor. This educational book for children uses silliness to show how compassion and inclusiveness impact our friendships and our lives. A must-have for early readers ages 6 to 10.

Paperback ISBN : 978-1-7327385-2-2
Hardback ISBN : 978-1-7327385-4-6
Library of Congress Control Number: 2019919587

Published by Chakra Publishing House LLC
West Windsor, NJ 08550
chakra.publishing.house@gmail.com

Dedicated to every parent who....

... did the right thing for their child knowing they faced a sub-optimal outcome for themselves
... checked out their ego and showered unconditional love towards their child
... taught their child to be kind by showing kindness towards them
... taught their child to be patient by first being patient themselves
... valued artistic freedom more than a clean table
... taught their child that being rich or poor had nothing to do with money
... taught their child that winning included showing compassion for an opponent
... taught their child that since we all begin and end as cosmic dust, materialistic pursuits are anything but material
... taught their child to speak for those who don't have a voice
... taught their child that the only way to receive more is to give more
... put their phone or device away when their child was seeking their presence
... gave their child the freedom to make their own mistakes
... did not pass on their own prejudices to their child
... hugged their child during a meltdown and reassured them it would all be okay
... allowed a child to be just that - a child
... patiently read all of the above and rolled your eyes (at least once)

MEET THE CHARACTERS

Miss English

Señor Diego

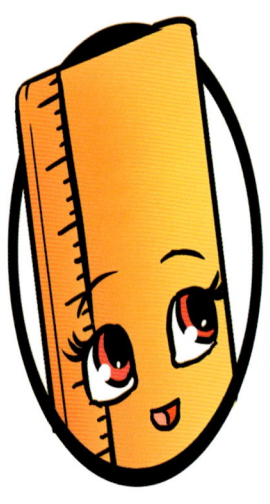

Mrs. Geetha

Once upon a time in Turning Corners Elementary School, it was the first day of school in 3rd Grade for A, E, I, O and U.

A, E, I, O and U had a busy first morning meeting their new teachers, learning a lot and then eating lunch. After lunch, they finally heard the announcement on the school radio they were all waiting for – LIBRARY. A, E, I, O and U headed straight to the library.

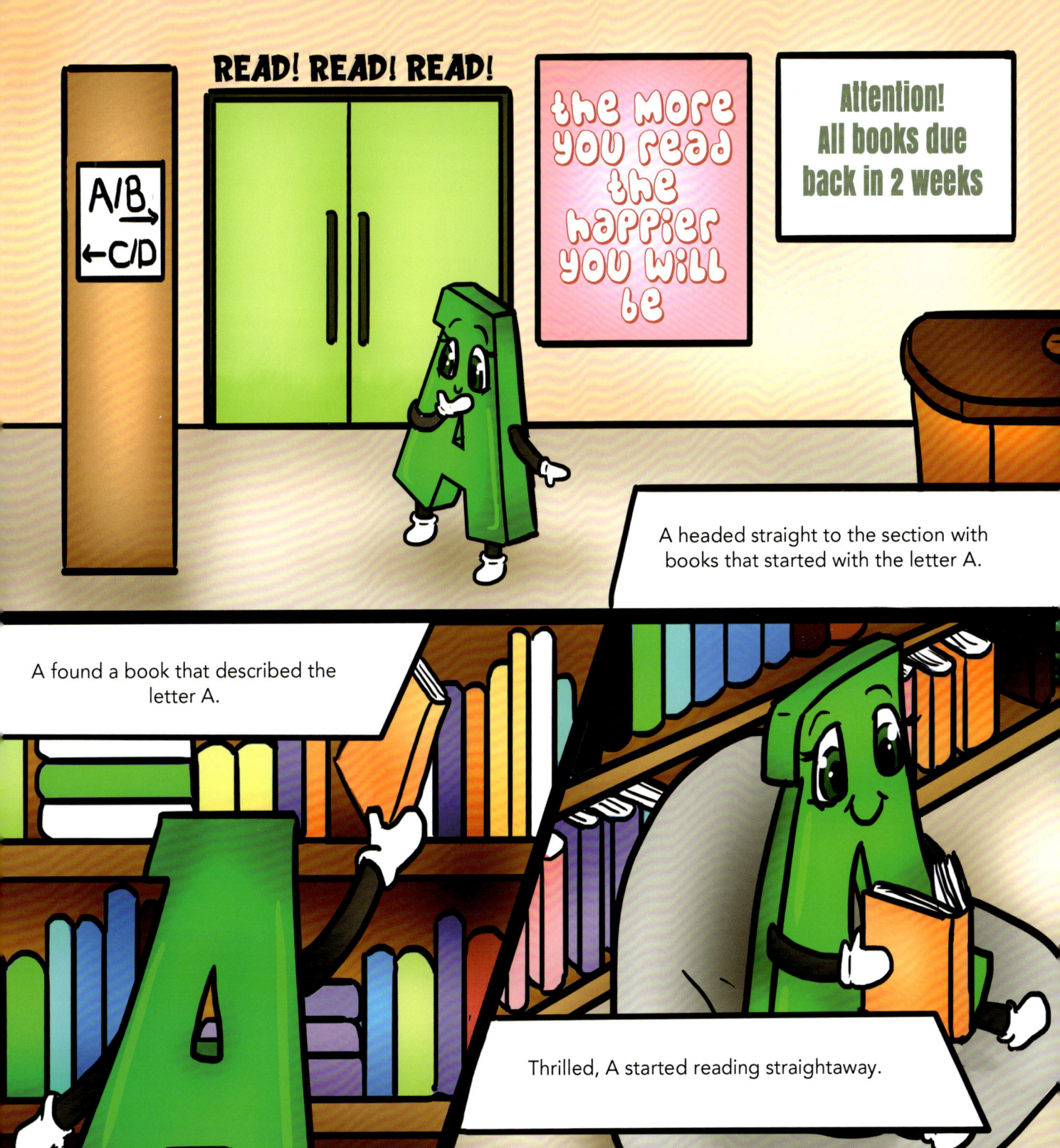

E, I, O and U ran to other sections of the library.

After reading on their own for some time, A, E, I, O and U met to share what they had learned.

A introduced itself first.

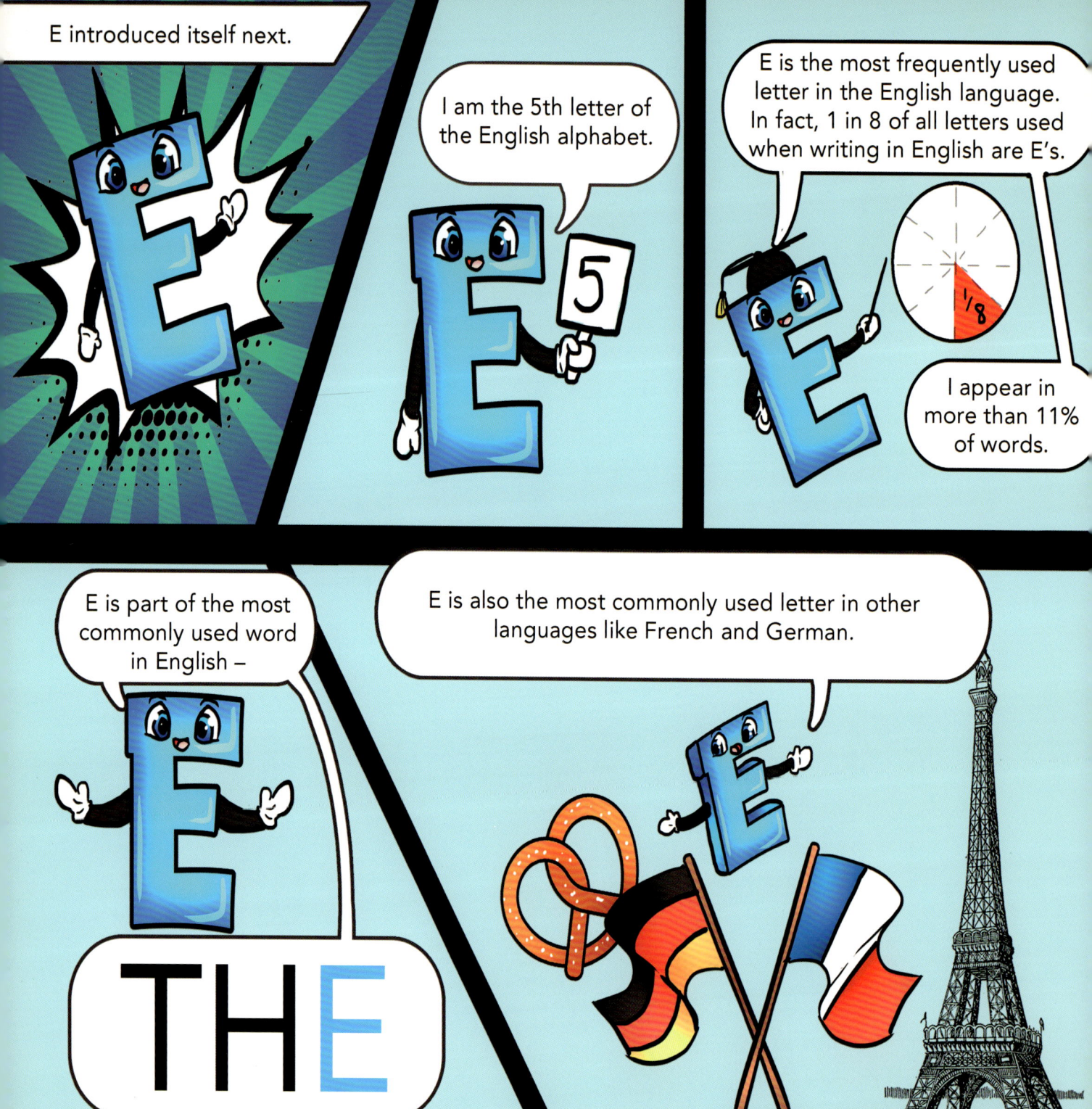

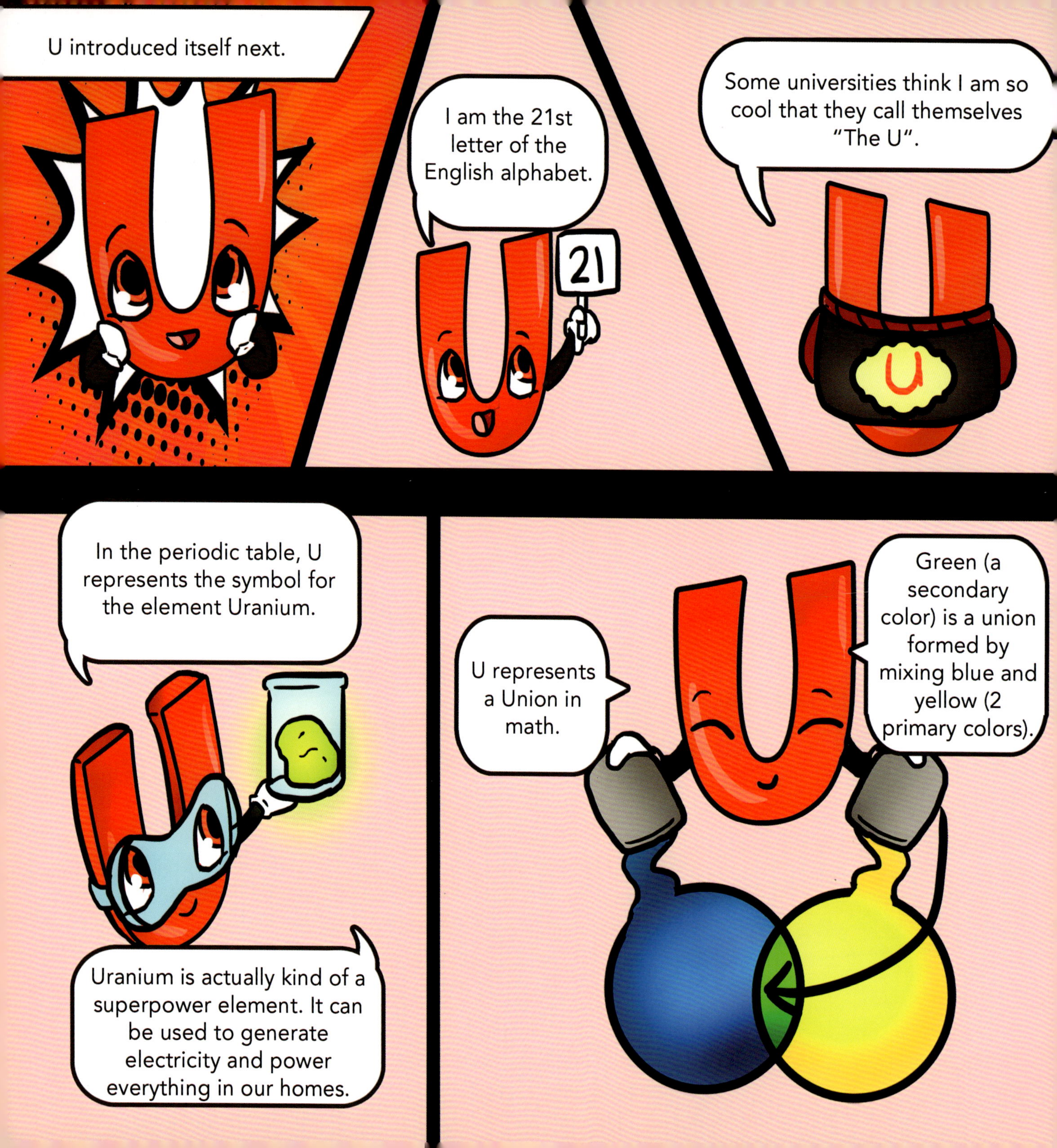

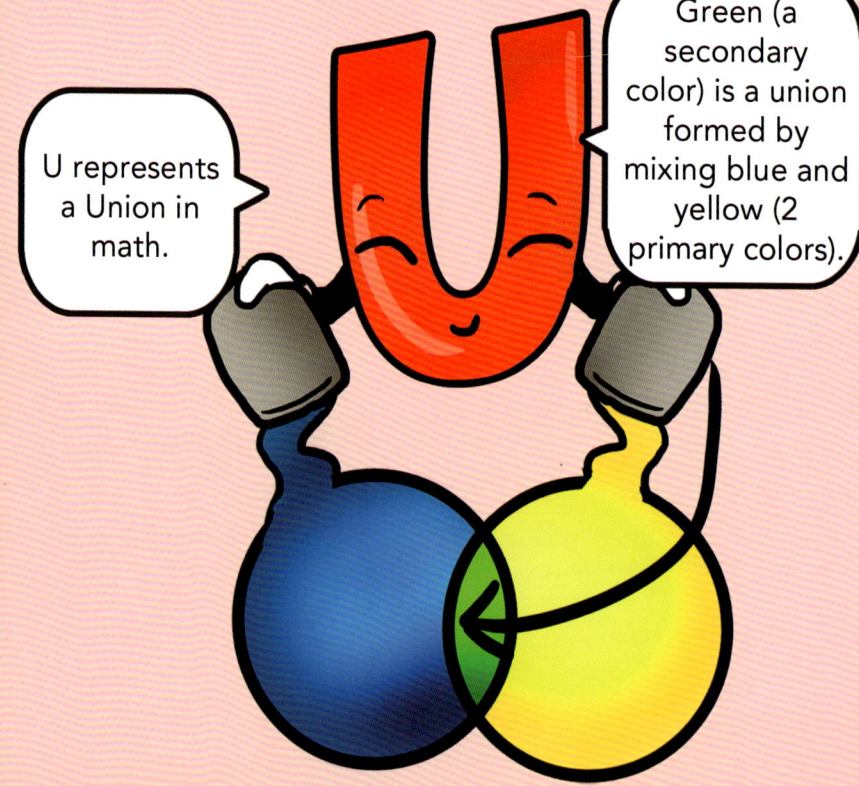

O introduced itself last.

Instead of talking about itself, O decided to talk about all the letters in the English language.

A, E, I, O and U are called vowels or speech sounds. The other 21 letters in the English language are called consonants.

Vowels have more than one sound or can be silent with no sound at all.

Y and W are also called semi-vowels as they can sound like a vowel or a consonant.

Here are some fun facts:

Ubkyh, a language with no native speakers today, has only 2 vowel sounds but 80+ consonants.

Sedang, a language spoken in Vietnam and Laos, has 24 vowels, the greatest number of vowels among all languages.

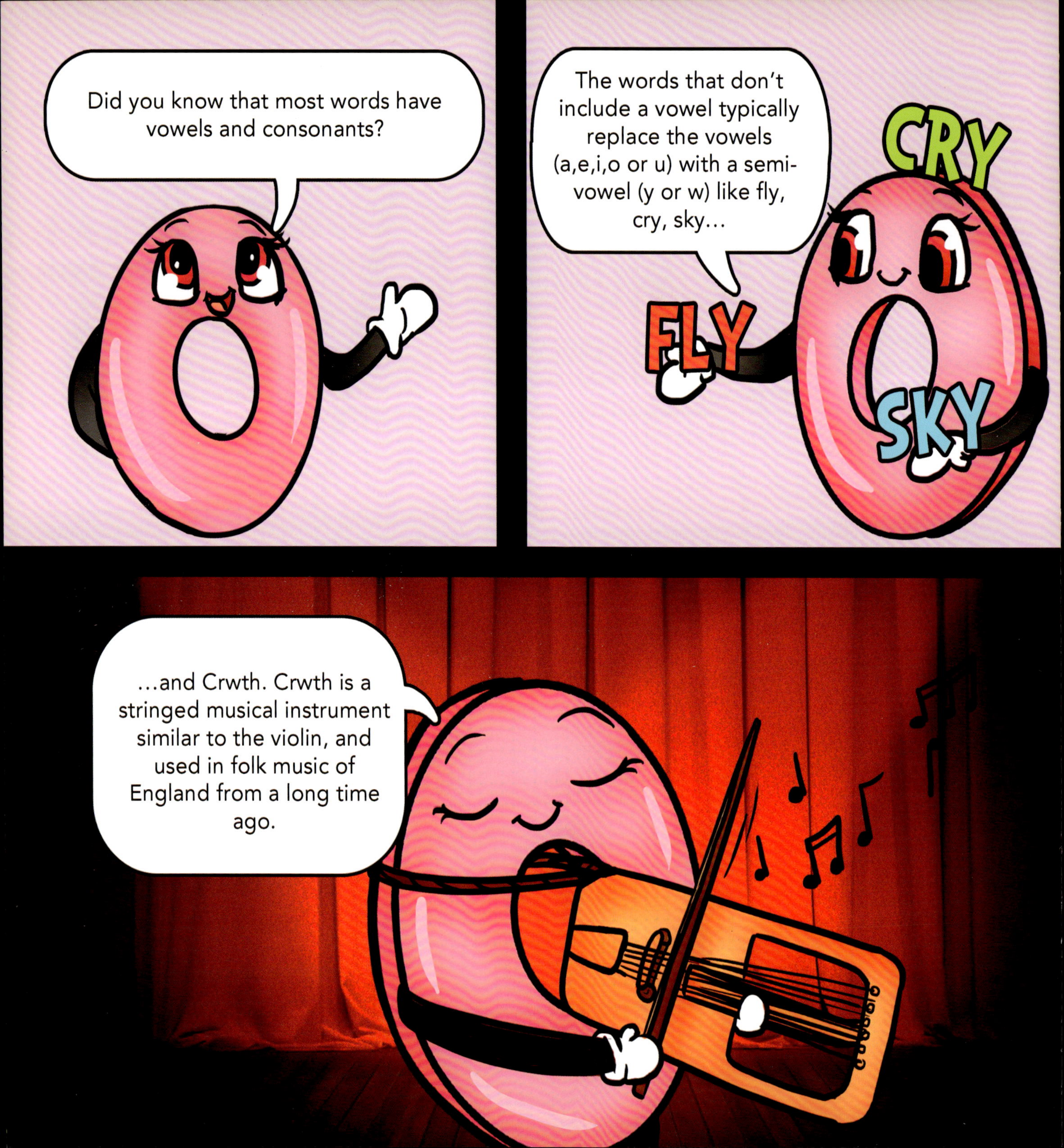

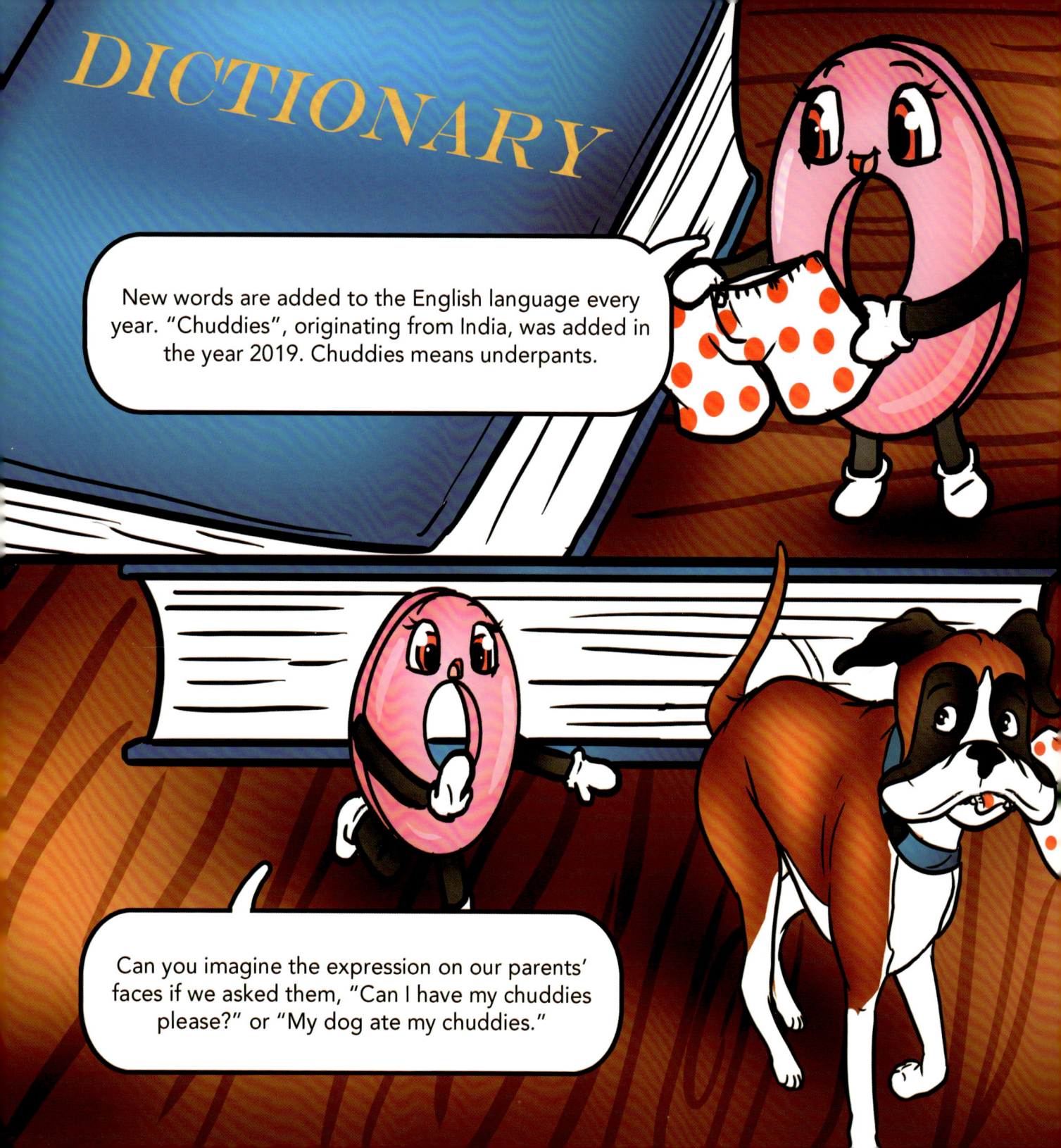

That evening, O went back home sad and told its mom everything that had happened in school that day.

O's mom told O that it was just the first day back in school and that O would make friends over time.

After dinner, O's mom tucked O into bed, and kissed O goodnight "Everything will be fine tomorrow."

The next morning, A, E, I, O and U woke up bright and early to get ready to go to school. They all took a shower and were ready for breakfast.

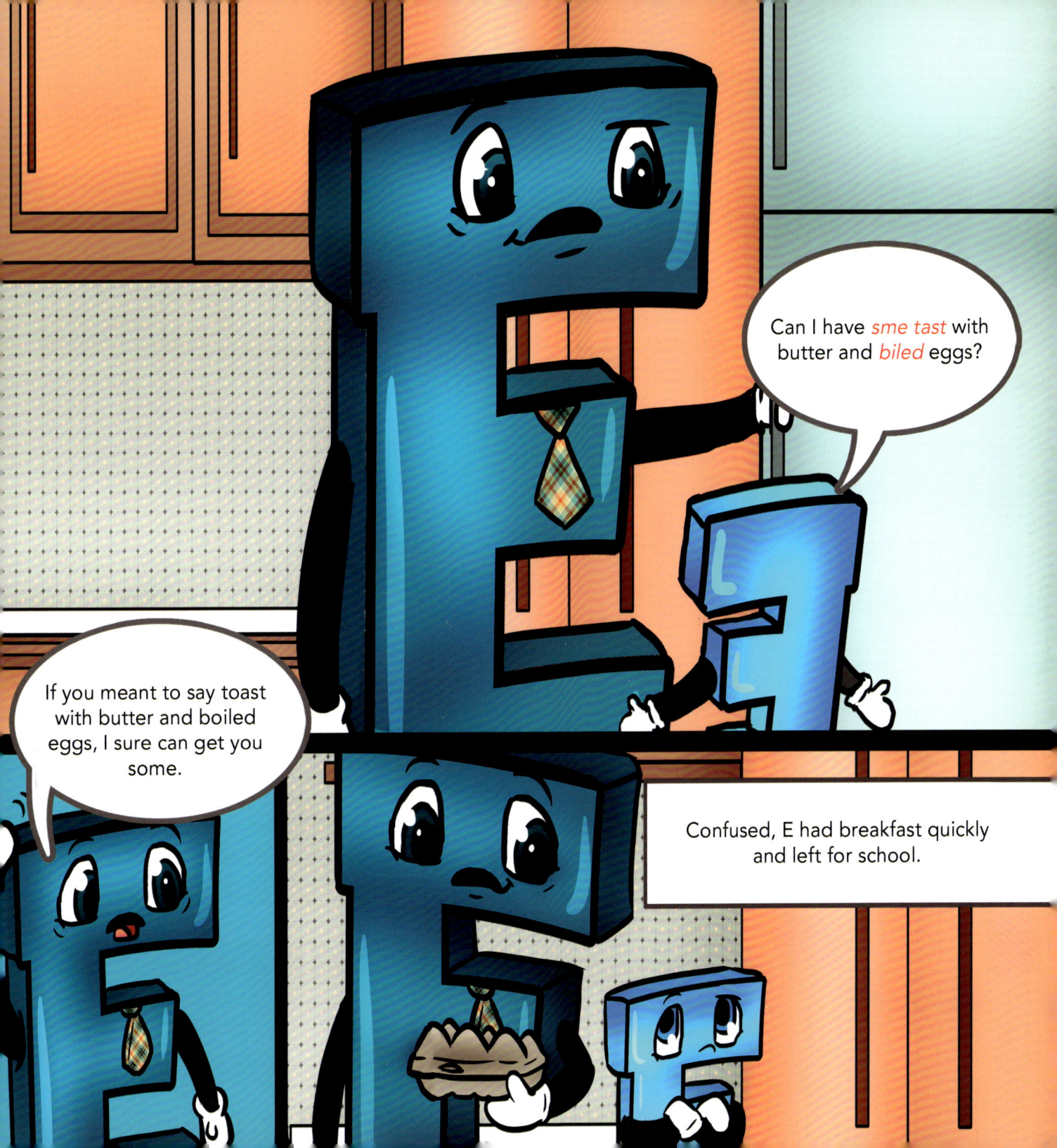

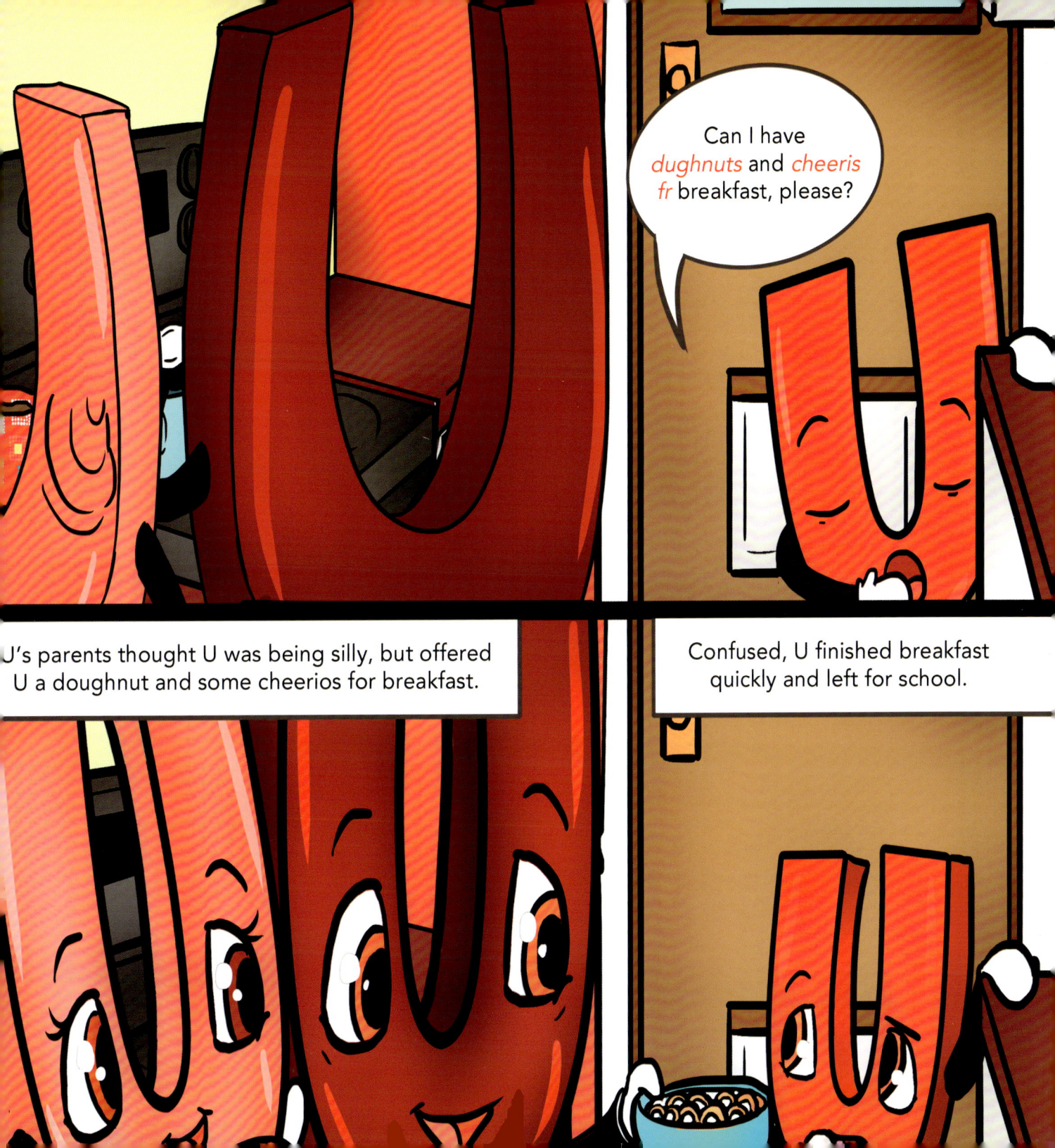

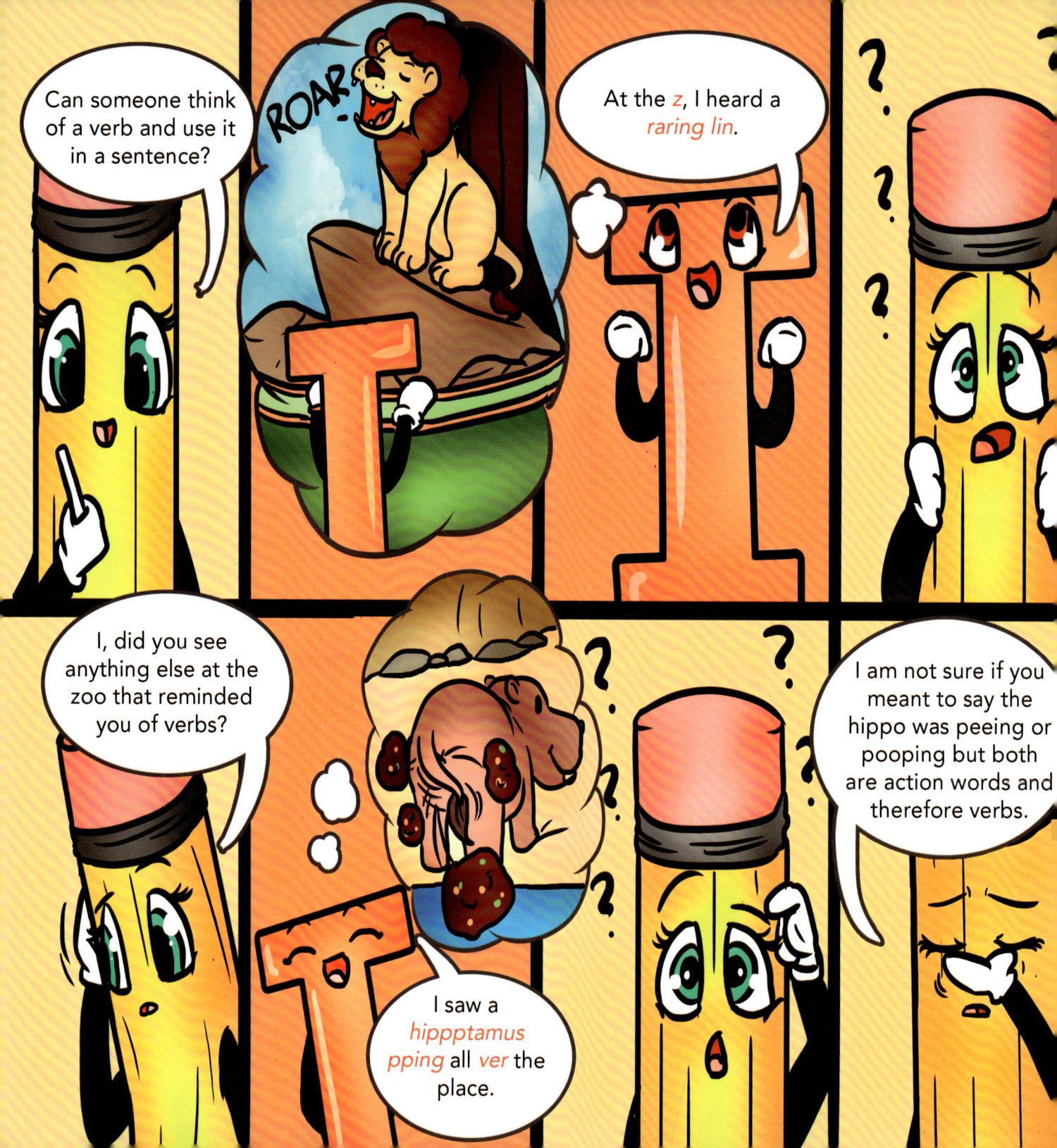

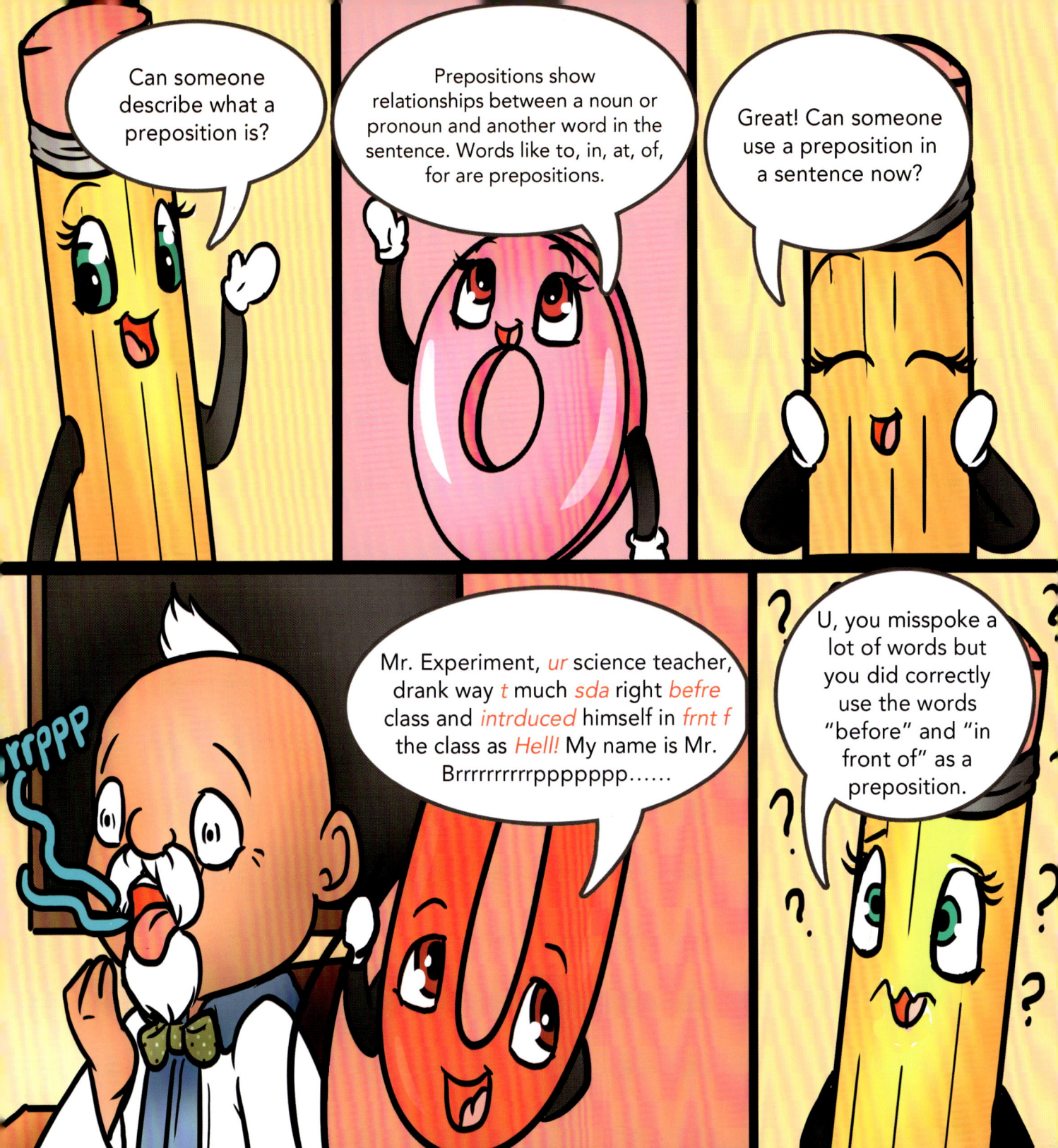

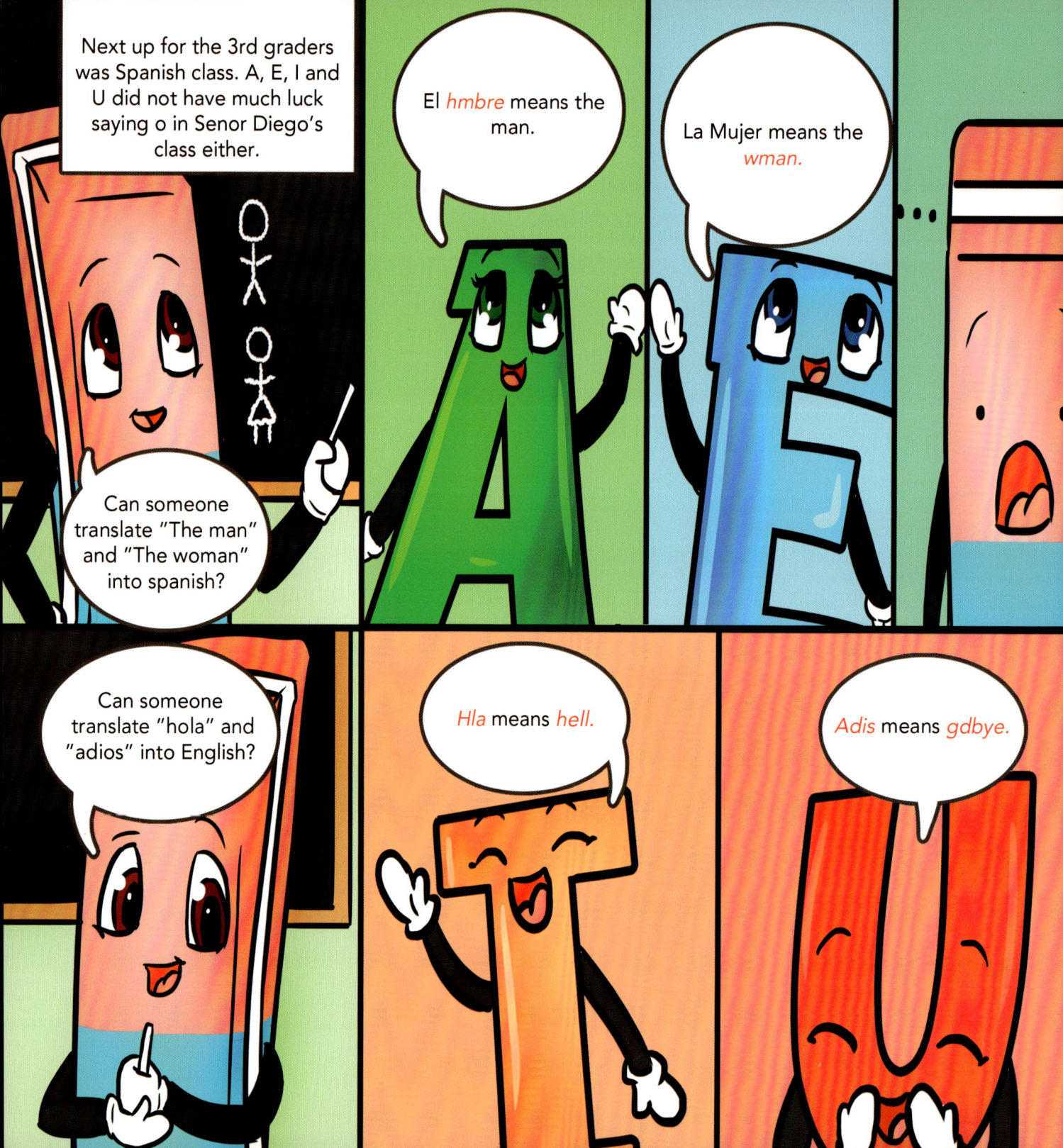

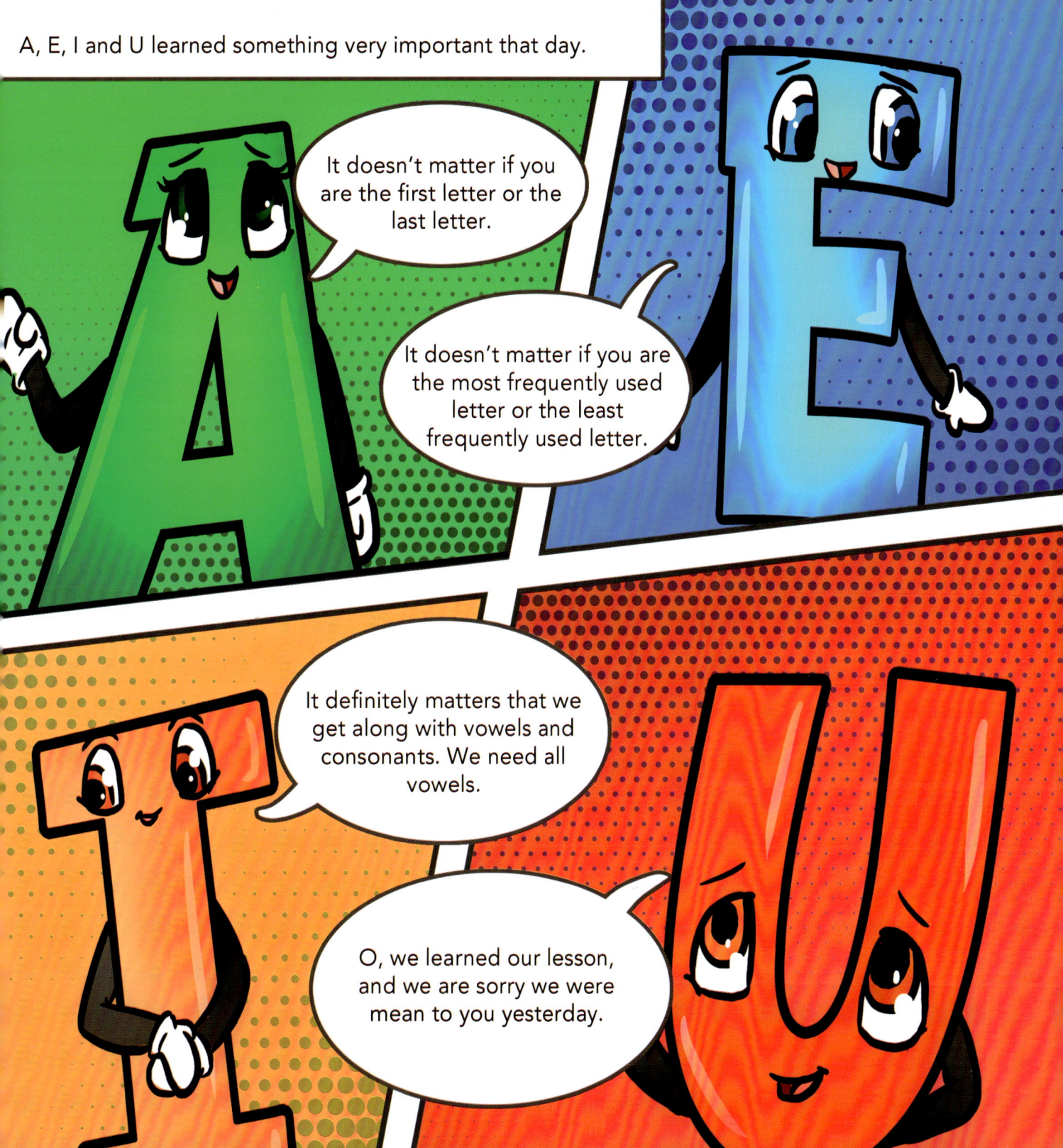

About the Family

The family that brought this book to life are Chakra Sreekanth (son), Sreekanth Kumar (father), and Sashi Sreekanth (mother). Chakra and Sreekanth are American writers of Indian origin. This father-and-son duo started working on this book when Chakra was in 2nd Grade. Sashi served as editor-in-chief giving the book its title and providing valuable insights in real-time. Most importantly, Sashi is the glue of the family keeping it real for her boys.

Chakra loves that his dad conjures up stories to make learning fun. With the help of his family, he wants to share these stories with the rest of the world. *All Vowels Matter* is one such story that highlights the importance of inclusion and acceptance. *All Vowels Matter* is the second installment in their series. The first is *All Shapes Matter* launched in September 2018. The family is currently working on their third book.